The Expulsive Power
of a New Affection

The Crossway Short Classics Series

Encouragement for the Depressed

CHARLES SPURGEON

The Expulsive Power of a New Affection

THOMAS CHALMERS

Heaven Is a World of Love

JONATHAN EDWARDS

THE EXPULSIVE
POWER OF A
NEW AFFECTION

THOMAS CHALMERS

WHEATON, ILLINOIS

The Expulsive Power of a New Affection

Copyright © 2020 by Crossway

Published by Crossway
1300 Crescent Street
Wheaton, Illinois 60187

Cover design: Jordan Singer

Cover image: "Marigold" wallpaper design, William Morris (1834–1896), Bridgeman Images

First printing 2020

Printed in China

Scripture quotations are from the King James Version of the Bible.

Paperback ISBN: 978-1-4335-7067-4
ePub ISBN: 978-1-4335-7070-4
PDF ISBN: 978-1-4335-7068-1
Mobipocket ISBN: 978-1-4335-7069-8

Library of Congress Cataloging-in-Publication Data

Names: Chalmers, Thomas, 1780–1847, author.
Title: The expulsive power of a new affection / Thomas Chalmers.
Description: Wheaton, Illinois: Crossway, 2020. | Series: The Crossway short classics series | Includes bibliographical references. |
Summary: "This book is a timeless treasure exhorting readers to remove the tangles of sin through the expulsive power of a new affection—desiring God"—Provided by publisher.
Identifiers: LCCN 2020005204 (print) | LCCN 2020005205 (ebook) | ISBN 9781433570674 (trade paperback) | ISBN 9781433570681 (pdf) | ISBN 9781433570698 (mobi) | ISBN 9781433570704 (epub)
Subjects: LCSH: Love—Religious aspects—Christianity—Sermons. | God—Worship and love—Sermons. | Sermons, English—19th century. | Bible. Epistles of John—Sermons.
Classification: LCC BX9178.C52 E9 2020 (print) | LCC BX9178.C52 (ebook) | DDC 248.4/852—dc23
LC record available at https://lccn.loc.gov/2020005204
LC ebook record available at https://lccn.loc.gov/2020005205

Crossway is a publishing ministry of Good News Publishers.

RRDS   28 27 26 25 24 23 22 21 20
14 13 12 11 10 9 8 7 6 5 4 3 2 1

Contents

Foreword by John Piper   9

Series Preface   17

Biography of Thomas Chalmers   21

The Expulsive Power of a New Affection   25

Foreword

WHO WAS THOMAS CHALMERS (1780–1847)? Converted to Christ while already in the pastorate (1810) in Kilmany, Scotland, Chalmers eventually became professor of moral philosophy in the University of St. Andrews, and then professor of theology in the University of Edinburgh.

His influence in the church and politics in Scotland was so extensive that according to geologist Hugh Miller, Chalmers "may be said rather to have *created* than to have *belonged* to an era."[1] And

---

1 Cited in Stuart C. Weir and John C. McDowell, *The Good Work of Non-Christians, Empowerment, and the New Creation: The Efficacy of the Holy Spirit's Empowering for Ordinary Work* (Eugene, OR: Pickwick, 2016), xxix.

William Gladstone, Britain's foremost political leader of the nineteenth century, called him "a man greatly lifted out of the region of mere flesh and blood."[2] On Chalmers's death, one estimate was that half the population of Edinburgh attended his funeral (p. 764).

During his professorship at St. Andrews, his passion for global missions was so inspiring that six of his best students dedicated themselves to missions, resulting in 141 years of combined missionary service.[3]

Though he was influential in geology and astronomy, Christian apologetics, relief for the poor, economics, Calvinistic orthodoxy, and ecclesias-

2 Mark Noll, "Thomas Chalmers (1780–1847) in North America (ca. 1830–1917)," in *Church History* 66, no. 4 (December 1997): 763. Emphasis added. All the page numbers in parentheses are from this article.

3 Stuart Piggin and John Foxborogh, *The St. Andrews Seven* (Edinburgh: Banner of Truth, 1985, 111.

tical leadership (helping create the Free Church of Scotland), nevertheless, it was the force of his words that gave effect to all of these engagements. According to A. C. Cheyne, his oratorical power "bordered on wizardry" (p. 764). William Wilberforce wrote in his diary in 1817, "All the world wild about Dr. Chalmers" (p. 762). But why? Princeton's James Alexander asked John Mason on his return from Scotland why Chalmers was so effective, and Mason replied, "It is his blood-earnestness."[4]

As you read this most famous sermon of Chalmers, "The Expulsive Power of a New Affection," I suggest you let that tone—blood-earnestness—shape the way you read. That is, don't think he is trifling. He is very serious. Joyfully serious.

I recall once being asked the trick question, If you had access to all the latest machinery in a

4   James W. Alexander, *Thoughts on Preaching* (Edinburgh: Banner of Truth, 1975), 264.

sophisticated science lab, what would be the most effective way to get all the air out of a glass beaker? One ponders the possible ways to force the air out. Then the answer is given: fill it with water.

That is the point of this sermon. It is intended as an illumination of 1 John 2:15, "Love not the world, neither the things that are in the world. If any man love the world, the love of the Father is not in him."

Chalmers poses for himself the question, How shall the human heart be freed from its *love* for the world? (How shall the air be removed from the beaker?) This "love" is not a duty one performs. It is a delight one prefers. It is an affection before it is a commitment.

He says there are two ways one might seek to remove this controlling affection from the heart. One is to show that the world is not worthy of our affection and will let us down in the end. (This argument corresponds to using a pump to suck the air out of the beaker.) The other is to show that God is vastly more worthy of the heart's attachment, thus awakening a new and stronger affection that displaces the former affection for the world. (This corresponds to pouring water into the beaker to displace the air.) Hence, "the expulsive power of a new affection."

Here's how Chalmers states his purpose:

My purpose is to show, that from the constitution of our nature, the former method is altogether incompetent and ineffectual and that the latter method will alone suffice for the rescue and recovery of the heart from the wrong affection that domineers over it.

Don't miss the words "from the constitution of our nature." He's going to make his point by arguing "from the constitution of our nature," not from an exposition of the biblical text. This is why I said above that this sermon (Or was it a lecture? We have lost the historical setting when it was delivered.) is intended as an *illumination* (not an exposition) of 1 John 2:15.

Chalmers could do biblical exposition. But he was a scientist and a philosopher, as well as a preacher of biblical texts. His apologetical contribution, which made him so popular in his day, was to show that biblical morality is rooted not just in religious authority, but in the profound realities of the way things really are in the world. This is what he means by saying that he is going to argue "from the constitution of our nature." In other words, he will appeal to what ordinary unbelievers can actually see about the way their heart works.

Without taking away the excitement of your own discovery of how Chalmers argues from the nature of our souls to the biblical reality of 1 John 2:15, I will give one enticement to ponder as you read. One of his central insights about the "constitution" of our nature is that nature hates a vacuum. This is why we can't displace the air in the beaker with a pump as easily as we can by pouring water in. The empty beaker fights back. It hates being empty. It demands content.

So it is with the human heart, Chalmers argues:

> Such is the grasping tendency of the human heart, that it must have a something to lay hold of—and which, if wrested away without the substitution of another something in its place, would leave a void and a vacancy as painful to the mind, as hunger is to the natural system.

This is why Chalmers thinks it is futile to try to suck sinful pleasures out of the human heart with the pump of fear, if we do not put a better pleasure in their place. One might think that humans have the capacity to use willpower and resolve to stop loving the world. But according to Chalmers, "The habit cannot so be displaced as to leave nothing but a negative and cheerless vacancy behind it." That, he argues, is "the constitution of our nature."

There is more, much more, as Chalmers penetrates into the nature of the human soul and the nature of regenerating grace. But if I keep on, I will spoil the quest. Perhaps you will decide, by the time you are done reading, that he has shed so much light on the workings of your own heart in relation to 1 John 2:15 that his *illumination* is, in fact, a very powerful *exposition* of God's meaning.

John Piper
Founder and teacher, desiringGod.org
Chancellor, Bethlehem College & Seminary

Series Preface

JOHN PIPER ONCE WROTE that books do not change people, but paragraphs do. This pithy statement gets close to the idea at the heart of the Crossway Short Classics series: some of the greatest and most powerful Christian messages are also some of the shortest and most accessible. The broad stream of confessional Christianity contains an astonishing wealth of timeless sermons, essays, lectures, and other short pieces of writing. These pieces have challenged, inspired, and borne fruit in the lives of millions of believers across church history and around the globe.

The Crossway Short Classics series seeks to serve two purposes. First, it aims to beautifully preserve these short historic pieces of writing through new high-quality physical editions. Second, it aims to transmit them to a new generation of readers, especially readers who may not be inclined or able to access a larger volume. Short-form content is especially valuable today, as the challenge of focusing in a distracting, constantly moving world becomes more intense. The volumes in the Short Classics series present incisive, gospel-centered grace and truth through a concise, memorable medium. By connecting readers with these accessible works, the Short Classics series hopes to introduce Christians to those great heroes of the faith who wrote them, providing readers with representative works that both nourish the soul and inspire further study.

Readers should note that the spelling and punctuation of these works have been lightly updated where applicable. Scripture references and other citations have also been added where appropriate. Language that reflects a work's origin as a sermon or public address has been retained. Our goal is to preserve as much as possible the authentic text of these classic works.

Our prayer is that the Holy Spirit will use these short works to arrest your attention, preach the gospel to your soul, and motivate you to continue exploring the treasure chest of church history, to the praise and glory of God in Christ.

Biography of
Thomas Chalmers

THOMAS CHALMERS (1780–1847) was born in Fife, Scotland. He desired the call of a minister early in life, becoming an ordained Presbyterian pastor before his twentieth birthday. Chalmers's intellectual gifts and rhetorical talent immediately gave him a reputation in his home parish as a powerful preacher.

However, it was not until reading the work of English evangelical and slavery abolitionist William Wilberforce that Chalmers was deeply convicted of his need for personal gospel faith and transformation. He was already serving as a pastor when he underwent this radical change in his theology, preaching, and life.

In 1843, Chalmers and several hundred other pastors in the Church of Scotland broke with the church over issues of ecclesiology. They formed the Free Church of Scotland, with Chalmers serving as its first moderator, a position he held until his death.

Though Chalmers was a brilliant scholar—he was the chair of moral philosophy at the University of St. Andrews for five years and was eventually named a fellow of the Royal Society of Edinburgh—his writing and preaching reflect most deeply an urgent desire for Christians to experience Christ's transformative power in all of life. He adamantly rejected the formalistic, unsupernatural theology of modernism that held sway with many in his time. He was a champion of the poor and actively engaged politics in the cause of poverty relief.

Much like his contemporaries Wilberforce and John Newton, Chalmers embraced a holistic view of the Christian life, exhorting believers to joyfully and sacrificially live out the life-changing implications of the gospel.

THE EXPULSIVE POWER OF A NEW AFFECTION

"Love not the world, neither the things that are in the world. If any man love the world, the love of the Father is not in him."

1 John 2:15

I

THERE ARE TWO WAYS in which a practical moralist may attempt to displace from the human heart its love of the world—either by a demonstration of the world's vanity, so as that the heart shall be prevailed upon simply to withdraw its regards from an object that is not worthy of it; or by setting forth another object, even God, as more worthy of its attachment, so as that the heart shall be prevailed upon not to resign an old affection, which shall have nothing to succeed it, but to exchange an old affection for a new one.

My purpose is to show that from the constitution of our nature, the former method is altogether incompetent and ineffectual, and that the latter method will alone suffice for the rescue and recovery of the heart from the wrong affection that domineers over it. After having accomplished this purpose, I shall attempt a few practical observations.

Love may be regarded in two different conditions. The first is when its object is at a distance, and then it becomes love in a state of desire. The second is when its object is in possession, and then it becomes love in a state of indulgence.

Under the impulse of desire, man feels himself urged onward in some path or pursuit of activity for its gratification. The faculties of his mind are put into busy exercise. In the steady direction of one great and engrossing interest, his attention is recalled from the many reveries into which it might otherwise have wandered; and the powers of his body are forced away from an indolence in which it else might have languished; and that time is crowded with occupation, which, but for some object of keen and devoted ambition, might have drivelled along in successive hours of weariness and distaste—and though hope does not always enliven, and success does not always crown this career of exertion, yet in the midst of this very variety, and with the alternations of occasional disappointment, is the machinery of the whole man kept in a sort of congenial play and upholden in that tone and temper that are most agreeable to it.

Insomuch that if, through the extirpation[1] of that desire that forms the originating principle of all this movement, the machinery were to stop and to receive no impulse from another desire substituted in its place, the man would be left with all his propensities to action in a state of most painful and unnatural abandonment. A

1   Elimination

sensitive being suffers and is in violence if, after having thoroughly rested from his fatigue or been relieved from his pain, he continues in possession of powers without any excitement to these powers; if he possesses a capacity of desire without having an object of desire; or if he has a spare energy upon his person without a counterpart and without a stimulus to call it into operation.

The misery of such a condition is often realized by him who is retired from business, retired from law, or even retired from the occupations of the chase and of the gaming table. Such is the demand of our nature for an object in pursuit that no accumulation of previous success can extinguish it—and thus it is that the most prosperous merchant and the most victorious general and the most fortunate gamester, when the labor of their respective vocations has come to a close, are often found to languish in the midst of all their acquisitions, as if out of their kindred and rejoicing element.

It is quite in vain, with such a constitutional appetite for employment in man, to attempt cutting away from him the spring or the principle of one employment without providing him with another. The whole heart and habit will rise in resistance against such an undertaking. The else unoccupied female who spends the hours of every evening at some play of hazard[2] knows as well as you that the pecuniary[3] gain or the honorable triumph of a successful contest are altogether paltry. It is not such a demonstration of vanity as this that will force her away from her dear and delightful occupation. The habit cannot so be displaced as to leave nothing but a negative and cheerless vacancy behind it—though it may so

2   A dice game
3   Financial

be supplanted as to be followed up by another habit of employment, to which the power of some new affection has constrained her. It is willingly suspended, for example, on any single evening, should the time that wont to be allotted to gaining require to be spent on the preparations of an approaching assembly. The ascendant power of a second affection will do what no exposition, however forcible, of the folly and worthlessness of the first ever could effectuate.

And it is the same in the great world. We shall never be able to arrest any of its leading pursuits by a naked demonstration of their vanity. It is quite in vain to think of stopping one of these pursuits in any way else but by stimulating to another. In attempting to bring a worldly man intent and busied with the prosecution of his objects to a dead stand, we have not merely to encounter the charm that he annexes to these objects—but we have to encounter the pleasure that he feels in the very prosecution of them. It is not enough, then, that we dissipate the charm by a moral and eloquent and affecting exposure of its illusiveness. We must address to the eye of his mind another object, with a charm powerful enough to dispossess the first of its influences and to engage him in some other prosecution as full of interest and hope and congenial activity as the former.

It is this that stamps an impotency on all moral and pathetic declamation about the insignificance of the world. A man will no more consent to the misery of being without an object because that object is a trifle, or of being without a pursuit because that pursuit terminates in some frivolous or fugitive acquirement, than he will voluntarily submit himself to the torture because that torture is to be of short duration.

If to be without desire and without exertion altogether is a state of violence and discomfort, then the present desire, with its correspondent train of exertion, is not to be got rid of simply by destroying it. It must be by substituting another desire and another line or habit of exertion in its place—and the most effectual way of withdrawing the mind from one object is not by turning it away upon desolate and unpeopled vacancy, but by presenting to its regards another object still more alluring.

These remarks apply not merely to love considered in its state of desire for an object not yet obtained. They apply also to love considered in its state of indulgence, or placid gratification, with an object already in possession. It is seldom that any of our tastes are made to disappear by a mere process of natural extinction. At least, it is very seldom that this is done through the instrumentality of reasoning. It may be done by excessive pampering—but it is almost never done by the mere force of mental determination. But what cannot be destroyed may be dispossessed, and one taste may be made to give way to another and to lose its power entirely as the reigning affection of the mind.

It is thus that the boy ceases, at length, to be the slave of his appetite, but it is because a manlier taste has now brought it into subordination; and that the youth ceases to idolize pleasure, but it is because the idol of wealth has become the stronger and gotten the ascendency; and that even the love of money ceases to have the mastery over the heart of many a thriving citizen, but it is because drawn into the whirl of city polities, another affection has been wrought into his moral system, and he is now lorded over by the love of power.

II

There is not one of these transformations in which the heart is left without an object. Its desire for one particular object may be conquered; but as to its desire for having some one object or other, this is unconquerable. Its adhesion to that on which it has fastened the preference of its regards cannot willingly be overcome by the rending away of a simple separation. It can be done only by the application of something else, to which it may feel the adhesion of a still stronger and more powerful preference.

Such is the grasping tendency of the human heart that it must have a something to lay hold of—and which, if wrested away without the substitution of another something in its place, would leave a void and a vacancy as painful to the mind as hunger is to the natural system. It may be dispossessed of one object or of any, but it cannot be desolated of all. Let there be a breathing and a sensitive heart, but without a liking and without affinity to any of the things that are around it, and, in a state of cheerless abandonment, it would be alive to nothing but the burden of its own consciousness and feel it to be intolerable. It would make no difference to its owner whether he dwelt in the midst of a gay and goodly world; or, placed afar beyond the outskirts of creation, he dwelt a solitary unit in dark and unpeopled nothingness. The heart must have something to cling to—and never, by its own voluntary consent, will it so denude itself of its attachments that there shall not be one remaining object that can draw or solicit it.

The misery of a heart thus bereft of all relish for that which wont to minister enjoyment is strikingly exemplified in those who, satiated with indulgence, have been so belabored, as it were, with the variety and the poignancy of the pleasurable sensations they have experienced that they are at length fatigued out of all capacity for sensation whatever. The disease of ennui is more frequent in the French metropolis, where amusement is more exclusively the occupation of the higher classes, than it is in the British metropolis, where the longings of the heart are more diversified by the resources of business and politics. There are the votaries of fashion, who, in this way, have at length become the victims of fashionable excess—in whom the very multitude of their enjoyments has at last extinguished their power of enjoyment; who, with the gratifications of art and nature at command, now look upon all that is around them with an eye of tastelessness; and who, plied with the delights of sense and of splendor even to weariness, and incapable of higher delights, have come to the end of all their perfection, and like Solomon of old, found it to be vanity and vexation.

The man whose heart has thus been turned into a desert can vouch for the insupportable languor that must ensue when one affection is thus plucked away from the bosom without another to replace it. It is not necessary that a man receive pain from anything in order to become miserable. It is barely enough that he looks with distaste to everything—and in that asylum that is the repository of minds out of joint, and where the organ of feeling as well as the organ of intellect has been impaired, it is not in the cell of loud and frantic outcries where we shall meet with the acme of mental suffering. But that is the individual who outpeers in wretchedness all his fellows, who, throughout the whole expanse of nature and society, meets not an object that has at all the power to detain or to interest him; who, neither in earth beneath nor in heaven above, knows of a single charm to which his heart can send forth one desirous or responding movement; to whom the world, in his eye a vast and empty desolation, has left him nothing but his own consciousness to feed upon, dead to all that is without him and alive to nothing but to the load of his own torpid and useless existence.

It will now be seen, perhaps, why it is that the heart keeps by its present affections with so much tenacity when the attempt is to do them away by a mere process of extirpation. It will not consent to be so desolated. The strong man, whose dwelling place is there, may be compelled to give way to another occupier—but unless another stronger than he has power to dispossess and to succeed him, he will keep his present lodgment inviolable. The heart would revolt against its own emptiness. It could not bear to be so left in a state of waste and cheerless insipidity. The moralist who tries such a process of dispossession as this upon the heart is thwarted at every step by the recoil of its own mechanism.

You have all heard that nature abhors a vacuum. Such at least is the nature of the heart, that though the room that is in it may change one inmate for another, it cannot be left void without the pain of most intolerable suffering. It is not enough then to argue the folly of an existing affection. It is not enough, in the terms of a forcible or an affecting demonstration, to make good the evanescence of its object. It may not even be enough to associate the threats and the terrors of some coming vengeance with the indulgence of it. The heart may still resist the every application, by obedience to which it would finally be conducted to a state so much at war with all its appetites as that of downright inanition.[4] So to tear away an affection from the heart, as to leave it bare of all its regards and of all its preferences, were a hard and hopeless undertaking—and it would appear as if the lone powerful engine of dispossession were to bring the mastery of another affection to bear upon it.

We know not a more sweeping interdict upon the affections of nature than that which is delivered by the apostle in the verse before us, 1 John 2:15. To bid a man into whom there has not yet entered the great and ascendant influence of the principle of regeneration, to bid him withdraw his love from all the things that are in the world, is to bid him give up all the affections that are in his heart. The world is the all of a natural man. He has not a taste or a desire that points not to a

4 Exhaustion

something placed within the confines of its visible horizon. He loves nothing above it and he cares for nothing beyond it, and to bid him love not the world is to pass a sentence of expulsion on all the inmates of his bosom. To estimate the magnitude and the difficulty of such a surrender, let us only think that it were just as arduous to prevail on him not to love wealth, which is but one of the things in the world, as to prevail on him to set willful fire to his own property. This he might do with sore and painful reluctance if he saw that the salvation of his life hung upon it. But this he would do willingly if he saw that a new property of tenfold value was instantly to emerge from the wreck of the old one.

In this case, there is something more than the mere displacement of an affection. There is the overbearing of one affection by another. But to desolate his heart of all love for the things of the world without the substitution of any love in its place were to him a process of as unnatural violence as to destroy all the things that he has in the world, and give him nothing in their room. So that, if to love not the world be indispensable to one's Christianity, then the crucifixion of the old man is not too strong a term to mark that transition in his history, when all old things are done away and all things become new.

III

We hope that by this time you understand the impotency of a mere demonstration of this world's insignificance. Its sole practical effect, if it had any, would be to leave the heart in a state that to every heart is insupportable, and that is a mere state of nakedness and negation. You may remember the fond and unbroken tenacity with which your heart has often recurred to pursuits, over the utter frivolity of which it sighed and wept but yesterday. The arithmetic of your short-lived days may on Sabbath make the clearest impression upon your understanding—and from his fancied bed of death, may the preacher cause a voice to descend in rebuke and mockery on all the pursuits of earthliness, and as he pictures before you the fleeting generations of men, with the absorbing grave, whither all the joys and interests of the world hasten to their sure and speedy oblivion, may you, touched and solemnized by his argument, feel for a moment as if on the eve of a practical and permanent emancipation from a scene of so much vanity.

But the morrow comes, and the business of the world and the objects of the world and the moving forces of the world come along with it—and the machinery of the heart, in virtue of which it must have something to grasp or something to adhere to, brings it under a kind of moral necessity to be actuated just as before. In utter repulsion toward a state so unkindly as that of being frozen out both of delight and of desire does it feel all the warmth and the urgency of its wonted solicitations—nor in the habit and history of the whole man can we detect so much as one symptom of the new creature—so that the church, instead of being to him a school of obedience, has been a mere sauntering place for the luxury of a passing and theatrical emotion; and the preaching that is mighty to compel the attendance of multitudes, that is mighty to still and to solemnize the hearers into a kind of tragic sensibility, that is mighty in the play of variety and vigor that it can keep up around the imagination, is not mighty to the pulling down of strongholds.

The love of the world cannot be expunged by a mere demonstration of the world's worthlessness.

But may it not be supplanted by the love of that which is more worthy than itself? The heart cannot be prevailed upon to part with the world by a simple act of resignation. But may not the heart be prevailed upon to admit into its preference another, who shall subordinate the world and bring it down from its wonted ascendancy? If the throne that is placed there must have an occupier, and the tyrant that now reigns has occupied it wrongfully, he may not leave a bosom that would rather detain him than be left in desolation. But may he not give way to the lawful sovereign, appearing with every charm that can secure his willing admittance and taking unto himself his great power to subdue the moral nature of man and to reign over it?

In a word, if the way to disengage the heart from the positive love of one great and ascendant object is to fasten it in positive love to another, then it is not by exposing the worthlessness of the former but by addressing to the mental eye the worth and excellence of the latter that all old things are to be done away and all things are to become new. To obliterate all our present affections by simply expunging them, and so as to leave the seat of them unoccupied, would be to destroy the old character and to substitute no new character in its place. But when they take their departure upon the ingress of other visitors; when they resign their sway to the power and the predominance of new affections; when, abandoning the heart to solitude, they merely give place to a successor who turns it into as busy a residence of desire and interest and expectation as before, there is nothing in all this to thwart or to overbear any of the laws of our sentient nature—and we see how, in fullest accordance with the mechanism of the heart, a great moral revolution may be made to take place upon it.

This, we trust, will explain the operation of that charm that accompanies the effectual preaching of the gospel. The love of God and the love of the world are two affections, not merely in a state of rivalship, but in a state of enmity—and that so irreconcilable that they cannot dwell together in the same bosom. We have already affirmed how impossible it were for the heart, by any innate elasticity of its own, to cast the world away from it and thus reduce itself to a wilderness. The heart is not so constituted, and the only way to dispossess it of an old affection is by the expulsive power of a new one. Nothing can exceed the magnitude of the required change in a man's character—when bidden as he is in the New Testament to love not the world, no, nor any of the things that are in the world, for this so comprehends all that is dear to him in existence as to be equivalent to a command of self-annihilation.

But the same revelation that dictates so mighty an obedience places within our reach as mighty an instrument of obedience. It brings for admittance to the very door of our heart an affection that, once seated upon its throne, will either subordinate every previous inmate or bid it away. Beside the world, it places before the eye of the mind him who made the world, and with this peculiarity, which is all its own—that in the gospel do we so behold God as that we may love God. It is there, and there only, where God stands revealed as an object of confidence to sinners, and where our desire after him is not chilled into apathy by that barrier of human guilt that intercepts every approach that is not made to him through the appointed Mediator. It is the bringing in of this better hope whereby we draw nigh unto God—

and to live without hope is to live without God; and if the heart be without God, the world will then have all the ascendancy.

It is God apprehended by the believer as God in Christ who alone can dispost it from this ascendancy. It is when he stands dismantled of the terrors that belong to him as an offended lawgiver and when we are enabled by faith, which is his own gift, to see his glory in the face of Jesus Christ and to hear his beseeching voice as it protests good will to men and entreats the return of all who will to a full pardon and a gracious acceptance, it is then that a love paramount to the love of the world, and at length expulsive of it, first arises in the regenerated bosom. It is when released from the spirit of bondage with which love cannot dwell, and when admitted into the number of God's children through the faith that is in Christ Jesus, the spirit of adoption is poured upon us—it is then that the heart, brought under the mastery of one great and predominant affection, is delivered from the tyranny of its former desires in the only way in which deliverance is possible. And that faith that is revealed to us from heaven as indispensable to a sinner's justification in the sight of God is also the instrument of the greatest of all moral and spiritual achievements on a nature dead to the influence and beyond the reach of every other application.

Thus may we come to perceive what it is that makes the most effective kind of preaching. It is not enough to hold out to the world's eye the mirror of its own imperfections. It is not enough to come forth with a demonstration, however pathetic, of the evanescent character of all its enjoyments. It is not enough to travel the walk of experience along with you and speak to your own conscience and your own recollection of the deceitfulness of the heart and the deceitfulness of all that the heart is set upon. There is many a bearer of the gospel message who has not shrewdness of natural discernment enough, and who has not power of characteristic description enough, and who has not the talent of moral delineation enough to present you with a vivid and faithful sketch of the existing follies of society. But that very corruption that he has not the faculty of representing in its visible details he may practically be the instrument of eradicating in its principle. Let him be but a faithful expounder of the gospel testimony, unable as he may be to apply a descriptive hand to the character of the present world; let him but report with accuracy the matter that revelation has brought to him from a distant world—unskilled as he is in the work of so anatomizing the heart, as with the power of a novelist to create a graphical or impressive exhibition of the worthlessness of its many affections; let him only deal in those mysteries of peculiar doctrine on which the best of novelists have thrown the wantonness of their derision.

He may not be able, with the eye of shrewd and satirical observation, to expose to the ready recognition of his hearers the desires of worldliness, but with the tidings of the gospel in commission, he may wield the only engine that can extirpate them. He cannot do what some have done, when, as if by the hand of a magician, they have brought out to view, from the hidden recesses of our nature, the foibles and lurking appetites that belong to it. But he has a truth in his possession, which into whatever heart it enters will, like the rod of Aaron, swallow up them all—and unqualified as he may be to describe the old man in all the nicer shading of his natural and constitutional varieties, with him is deposited that ascendant influence under which the leading tastes and tendencies of the old man are destroyed and he becomes a new creature in Jesus Christ our Lord.

Let us not cease then to ply the only instrument of powerful and positive operation to do away from you the love of the world. Let us try every legitimate method of finding access to your hearts for the love of him who is greater than the world. For this purpose, let us, if possible, clear away that shroud of unbelief that so hides and darkens the face of the Deity. Let us insist on his claims to your affection—and whether in the shape of gratitude or in the shape of esteem, let us never cease to affirm that in the whole of that wondrous economy, the purpose of which is to reclaim a sinful world unto himself, he, the God of love, so sets himself forth in characters of endearment that naught but faith and naught but

understanding are wanting, on your part, to call
forth the love of your hearts back again.

And here let us advert to the incredulity of
a worldly man: when he brings his own sound
and secular experience to bear upon the high
doctrines of Christianity—when he looks on regeneration as a thing impossible—when feeling
as he does the obstinacies of his own heart on
the side of things present, and casting an intel-
ligent eye, much exercised perhaps in the observation of human life, on the equal obstinacies
of all who are around him, he pronounces this
whole matter about the crucifixion of the old
man and the resurrection of a new man in his
place to be in downright opposition to all that
is known and witnessed of the real nature of hu-
manity. We think that we have seen such men,
who, firmly trenched in their own vigorous and
homebred sagacity, and shrewdly regardful of all

that passes before them through the week and upon the scenes of ordinary business, look on that transition of the heart by which it gradually dies unto time and awakens in all the life of a new-felt and ever-growing desire toward God as a mere Sabbath speculation; and who thus, with all their attention engrossed upon the concerns of earthliness, continue unmoved, to the end of their days, amongst the feelings and the appetites and the pursuits of earthliness.

If the thought of death, and another state of being after it, comes across them at all, it is not with a change so radical as that of being born again that they ever connect the idea of preparation. They have some vague conception of its being quite enough that they acquit themselves in some decent and tolerable way of their relative obligations; and that, upon the strength of some such social and domestic moralities as are often realized by him into whose heart the love of God has never entered, they will be transplanted in safety from this world, where God is the Being with whom it may almost be said that they have had nothing to do, to that world where God is the Being with whom they will have mainly and immediately to do throughout all eternity. They admit all that is said of the utter vanity of time when taken up with as a resting place. But they resist every application made upon the heart of man, with the view of so shifting its tendencies that it shall not henceforth find in the interests of time all its rest and all its refreshment.

They, in fact, regard such an attempt as an enterprise that is altogether aerial—and with a tone of secular wisdom, caught from the familiarities of everyday experience, do they see a visionary character in all that is said of setting our affections on the things that are above; and of walking by faith; and of keeping our hearts—in such a love of God as shall shut out from them the love of the world; and of having no confidence in the flesh; and of so renouncing earthly things as to have our conversation in heaven.

IV

Now it is altogether worthy of being remarked of those men who thus disrelish spiritual Christianity and, in fact, deem it an impracticable acquirement how much of a piece their incredulity about the demands of Christianity and their incredulity about the doctrines of Christianity are with one another. No wonder that they feel the work of the New Testament to be beyond their strength, so long as they hold the words of the New Testament to be beneath their attention. Neither they nor anyone else can dispossess the heart of an old affection but by the expulsive power of a new one—and, if that new affection be the love of God, neither they nor anyone else can be made to entertain it but on such a representation of the Deity as shall draw the heart of the sinner toward him.

Now it is just their unbelief that screens from the discernment of their minds this representation. They do not see the love of God in sending his Son unto the world. They do not see the expression of his tenderness to men in sparing him not, but giving him up unto the death for us all. They do not see the sufficiency of the atonement or the sufferings that were endured by him who bore the burden that sinners should have borne. They do not see the blended holiness and compassion of the Godhead, in that he passed by the transgressions of his creatures, yet could not pass them by without an expiation. It is a mystery to them how a man should pass to the state of godliness from a state of nature—but had they only a believing view of God manifest in the flesh, this would resolve for them the whole mystery of godliness. As it is, they cannot get quit of their old affections, because they are out of sight from all those truths that have influence to raise a new one. They are like the children of Israel in the land of Egypt, when required to make bricks without straw—they cannot love God while they want the only food that can aliment this affection in a sinner's bosom—and however great their errors may be both in resisting the demands of the gospel as impracticable and in rejecting the doctrines of the gospel as inadmissible, yet there is not a spiritual man (and it is the prerogative of him who is spiritual to judge all men) who will not perceive that there is a consistency in these errors.

But if there be a consistency in the errors, in like manner is there a consistency in the truths that are opposite to them. The man who believes in the peculiar doctrines will readily bow to the peculiar demands of Christianity. When he is told to love God supremely, this may startle another, but it will not startle him to whom God has been revealed in peace and in pardon and in all the freeness of an offered reconciliation. When told to shut out the world from his heart, this may be impossible with him who has nothing to replace it—but not impossible with him who has found in God a sure and a satisfying portion. When told to withdraw his affections from the things that are beneath, this were laying an order of self-extinction upon the man who knows not another quarter in the whole sphere of his contemplation to which he could transfer them—but it were not grievous to him whose view has been opened up to the loveliness and glory of the things that are above, and can there find for every feeling of his soul a most ample and delighted occupation. When told to look not to the things that are seen and temporal, this were blotting out the light of all that is visible from the prospect of him in whose eye there is a wall of partition between guilty nature and the joys of eternity—but he who believes that Christ hath broken down this wall finds a gathering radiance upon his soul as he looks onward in faith to the things that are unseen and eternal. Tell a man to be holy, and how can he compass such a performance when his alone fellowship with holiness is a fellowship of despair? It is the atonement of the cross reconciling the holiness of the lawgiver with the safety of the offender that hath opened the way for a sanctifying influence into the sinner's heart, and he can take a kindred impression from the character of God now brought nigh and now at peace with him. Separate the demand from the doctrine and you have either a system of righteousness that is impracticable or a barren orthodoxy. Bring the demand and the doctrine together, and the true disciple of Christ is able to do the one through the other strengthening him. The motive is adequate to the movement, and the bidden obedience of the gospel is not beyond the measure of his strength just because the doctrine of the gospel is not beyond the measure of his acceptance. The shield of faith and the hope of salvation and the Word of God and the girdle of truth—these are the armor that he has put on; and with these the battle is won and the eminence is reached and the man stands on the vantage ground of a new field and a new prospect. The effect is great, but the cause is equal to it—and stupendous as this moral resurrection to the precepts of Christianity undoubtedly is, there is an element of strength enough to give it being and continuance in the principles of Christianity. The object of the gospel is both to pacify the sinner's conscience and to purify his heart; and it is of importance to observe that what mars the one of these objects mars the other also. The best way of casting out an impure affection is to admit a pure one, and, by the love of what is good, to expel the love of what is evil.

Thus it is that the freer the gospel, the more sanctifying is the gospel; and the more it is received as a doctrine of grace, the more will it be felt as a doctrine according to godliness. This is one of the secrets of the Christian life, that the more a man holds of God as a pensioner, the greater is the payment of service that he renders back again. On the tenure of "Do this and live," a spirit of fearfulness is sure to enter; and the jealousies of a legal bargain chase away all confidence from the intercourse between God and man; and the creature, striving to be square and even with his Creator, is, in fact, pursuing all the while his own selfishness instead of God's glory; and with all the conformities that he labors to accomplish, the soul of obedience is not there, the mind is not subject to the law of God, nor indeed under such an economy ever can be. It is only when, as in the gospel, acceptance is bestowed as a present, without money and without price, that the security that man feels in God is placed beyond the reach of disturbance—or, that he can repose in him, as one friend reposes in another; or, that any liberal and generous understanding can be established betwixt them, the one party rejoicing over the other to do him good, the other finding that the truest gladness of his heart lies in the impulse of a gratitude by which it is awakened to the charms of a new moral existence.

Salvation by grace—salvation by free grace—salvation not of works, but according to the mercy of God—salvation on such a footing is not more indispensable to the deliverance of our persons from the hand of justice than it is to the deliverance of our hearts from the chill and the weight of ungodliness. Retain a single shred or fragment of legality with the gospel and we raise a topic of distrust between man and God. We take away from the power of the gospel to melt and to conciliate. For this purpose, the freer it is, the better it is. That very peculiarity that so many dread as the germ of antinomianism is, in fact, the germ of a new spirit and a new inclination against it. Along with the light of a free gospel does there enter the love of the gospel, which, in proportion as we impair the freeness, we are sure to chase away. And never does the sinner find within himself so mighty a moral transformation as when, under the belief that he is saved by grace, he feels constrained thereby to offer his heart a devoted thing and to deny ungodliness. To do any work in the best manner, we should make use of the fittest tools for it.

And we trust that what has been said may serve in some degree for the practical guidance of those who would like to reach the great moral achievement of our text—but feel that the tendencies and desires of nature are too strong for them. We know of no other way by which to keep the love of the world out of our hearts than to keep in our hearts the love of God—and no other way by which to keep our hearts in the love of God than building ourselves up on our most holy faith. That denial of the world that is not possible to him that dissents from the gospel testimony is possible, even as all things are possible, to him that believeth. To try this without faith is to work without the right tool or the right instrument.

But faith worketh by love, and the way of expelling from the heart the love that transgresseth the law is to admit into its receptacles the love that fulfilleth the law.

Conceive a man to be standing on the margin of this green world; and that, when he looked toward it, he saw abundance smiling upon every field, and all the blessings that earth can afford scattered in profusion throughout every family, and the light of the sun sweetly resting upon all the pleasant habitations, and the joys of human companionship brightening many a happy circle of society—conceive this to be the general character of the scene upon one side of his contemplation; and that, on the other, beyond the verge of the godly planet on which he was situated, he could descry nothing but a dark and fathomless unknown. Think you that he would bid a voluntary adieu to all the brightness and all the beauty that were before him upon earth, and commit himself to the frightful solitude away from it? Would he leave its peopled dwelling places and become a solitary wanderer through the fields of nonentity? If space offered him nothing but a wilderness, would he for it abandon the homebred scenes of life and of cheerfulness that lay so near and exerted such a power of urgency to detain him? Would not he cling to the regions of sense, and of life, and of society, and shrinking away from the desolation that was beyond it, would not he be glad to keep his firm footing on the territory of this world and to take shelter under the silver canopy that was stretched over it? But if, during the time of his contemplation, some happy island of the blest had floated by, and there had burst upon his senses the light of its surpassing glories and its sounds of sweeter melody—and he clearly saw that there a purer beauty rested upon every field and a more

heartfelt joy spread itself among all the families;
and he could discern there a peace and a piety and
a benevolence that put a moral gladness into every
bosom and united the whole society in one rejoicing sympathy with each other and with the benefi-
cent Father of them all; and could he further see
that pain and mortality were there unknown; and
above all, that signals of welcome were hung out,
and an avenue of communication was made for
him—perceive you not that what was before the
wilderness would become the land of invitation,
and that now the world would be the wilderness?

What unpeopled space could not do can be
done by space teeming with beatific scenes and
beatific society. And let the existing tendencies
of the heart be what they may to the scene that is
near and visibly around us, still if another stood
revealed to the prospect of man, either through
the channel of faith or through the channel of

his senses, then, without violence done to the constitution of his moral nature, may he die unto the present world and live to the lovelier world that stands in the distance away from it.